Tammye

Wow continue u

Keep Love alive

Latimy Smith

Lotario's Love Notes

Lotario's Love Notes

by

Lotario D. Jointer

An Ordinary Man with Extraordinary Experiences in Love.

Copyright © 2011 by Lotario D. Jointer

All rights reserved.

No part of this book shall be reproduced, stored in a retrieval system, or transmitted by any means without written permission from the author.

ISBN: 978-1-4583-7769-2

Scripture quotations taken from the New American Standard Bible®, Copyright © 1960, 1962, 1963, 1968, 1971, 1972, 1973, 1975, 1977, 1995 by The Lockman Foundation Used by permission. (www.Lockman.org)

Cover and book design by Fenesha N. Hubbard.

I dedicate this book to my father and mother--
It was because of the love they shared that I exist.

Honor your father and your mother,
that your days may be prolonged
in the land which the Lord your God gives you.

(Exodus 20:12)

This book is typeset in the Garamond font family and Jellyka.
The Jellyka Love and Passion font is courtesy of Jellyka Nerevan of

http://www.cuttyfruty.com and jellyka+daf@gmail.com

Contents

Note to Reader

Loving Life
1

Loving Self
25

In Between Loves
51

Between Lovers
73

Acknowledgments
Author's Page

If I have the gift of prophecy, and know all mysteries and all knowledge; and if I have all faith, so as to remove mountains, but do not have love, I am nothing.

And if I give all my possessions to feed the poor, and if I surrender my body to be burned, but do not have love, it profits me nothing.

Love is patient, love is kind and is not jealous; love does not brag and is not arrogant, does not act unbecomingly; it does not seek its own, is not provoked, does not take into account a wrong suffered, does not rejoice in unrighteousness, but rejoices with the truth; bears all things, believes all things, hopes all things, endures all things.

Love never fails; but if there are gifts of prophecy, they will be done away; if there are tongues, they will cease; if there is knowledge, it will be done away.

(1 Corinthians 13:2-8)

NOTE TO READER

Dear Reader,

I am an ordinary man, but I've had extraordinary experiences in **love**. I've been in **love**, out of **love**, hurt by what I thought was **love**, and committed to **love**. Through it all, my greatest lesson was to **love** without encouragement. I had to learn to **love** myself in order to **love** another person.

I began sharing **love** notes with friends who had weary spirits with broken hearts and had given up on **love**. Heartaches make you want to run from **love**, but we can't get away from **love** even if we try. **Love** is everywhere. So, I went inside of me and found some **love** to share with others so that they could believe again.

We all need and want **love**. Everyone would like to be hugged and held in high regard. We desire to be on our lover's mind as they rise to greet the new day, and at night when their head meets the pillow. We all want to experience **love**.

Perhaps you want to be in **love**, rekindle a **love** that was thought to be lost, or sustain the **love** you have right now. My **love** notes will provoke you to think about how you define and experience **love**. I've included **love** tips to inspire you to act on **love**, and journal pages to encourage you to reflect on **love**.

Thank you for reading. **Love** is you.

With **love**,

Lotario D. Jointer

*And so faith, hope, love, abide these three;
but the greatest of these is love.*

(1 Corinthians 13:13)

Loving Life

#1

Love believes in unlimited possibilities.

Love Tip:
Believe in love. Anything is possible.

#2

Love and fear cannot coexist.
Love is of God. Fear is of the devil.
Do you really want them in the same space?

Love Tip:
Clear out your space for love.

#3

Love is never produced in the devil's workshop because **love** cannot sit idly.

Love Tip:
Let love move you.

#4

Love doesn't hurt people. Hurt people hurt people.

Love Tip:
Love those that are hurt.

#5

Love is what **love** does.
Sometimes **love** does not do; but when it does, it never fails.

Love Tip:
Choose to love.

#6

Love lives in the moment.

Love Tip:
Be fully present with your presence.

Love Note
#7

Love doesn't allow your fears and insecurities to pose as logical choices.

Love Tip:
Take off the mask.

Love Note
#8

Love knows that you become filled
with gratitude each time you conquer a fear.

Love Tip:
Face your fears.

#9

Love is infinite;
it will go on with or without your participation.

Love Tip:
Surrender to love.

Love Note
#10

Love knows that the only tragedy in death is not having lived your life to the fullest.

Love Tip:
Live a life of love.

#11

Loving daily will be your legacy.

Love Tip:
Make it your intention to leave a legacy of love.

Love Note
#12

Love is like

Opening an

explosi**V**e

m**E**ssage.

Love Tip:
Love life so much that it detonates your love.

Describe a time when you believed in love.

Love Tip:
Believe in love.
Anything is possible.

Write down the things you need to remove from your life.

Love Tip:
Clear out your space for love.

When was the last time you moved beyond your comfort zone?

Love Tip:
Let love move you.

Whom do you need to forgive?

Love Tip:
Love those that are hurt.

List the people with whom you want to spend more time.

Love Tip:
Choose to love.

Make a list of the things you've been putting off to do later.

Love Tip:
Be fully present with your presence.

List your greatest fears.

Love Tip:
Face your fears.

List the things that you can improve upon.

Love Tip:
Live a life of love.

Why do you love life?

Love Tip:
Love life so much that it detonates your love.

Loving Self

#13

Love is a personal commitment.

Love Tip:
Love yourself so that you are able to love others.

#14

You **EVOL**ved from **LOVE**.

Love Tip:
Be love. Be you.

#15

You **love** yourself when you can say,
"I am the one who summoned this **love**."

Love Tip:
In some instances, love has to be about you.

#16

Love shelters you from those who choose to neglect **love**.

Love Tip:
Come out of hiding and face the truth.

#17

Love fills up the empty places masquerading as loneliness.

Love Tip:
Always surround yourself with positive people.

#18

Love knows that the right amount
of pain brings self-correction.

Love Tip:
If you burned your hand on a hot stove,
would you expect a different result
the next time you touch a hot stove?

#19

Self-**love** doesn't allow you to be the reason for your tears.

Love Tip:
Give yourself permission to cry.

#20

Loving you means being happy in your own skin.

Love Tip:
Remember that physical beauty is skin deep,
but spiritual beauty comes from love.

#21

Loving you means that **love** is your color, shape and size.

Love Tip:
Love your body.

#22

Before you can become an ambassador for self,
you must first fill your internal embassy with **love**.

Love Tip:
Be an ambassador of self-love.

Love Note
#23

Love meets most of your wants and all of your needs.

Love Tip:
Prioritize your life.

Love Note
#24

Love knows that you define your material things; they don't define you.

Love Tip:
You can't buy love.

#25

Love balances the spiritual, emotional and physical self.

Love Tip:
Love is the great equalizer.

#26

Your **love** is needed as a present
to those who come into your presence.

Love Tip:
Withholding your love will only hurt you.

Love Note
#27

Love understands that the advice
you choose to follow agrees with
the actions you were already willing to take.

Love Tip:
Take advice from one who has
successfully learned the love lesson.

Love Note
#28

Love is omnipresent and timeless,
but it will run away from those
that don't make time to **love** themselves.

Love Tip:
Make time just for you each day.

List the things that you can do daily to re-energize yourself.

Love Tip:
In some instances, love has to be about you.

I love my body because ...

Love Tip:
Love your body.

Who are the positive people in your life?

Love Tip: Always surround yourself with positive people.

List the mistakes for which you need to forgive yourself.

> **Love Tip:**
> If you burned your hand on a hot stove, would you expect a different result the next time you touch a hot stove?

List some things that have made you cry.

Love Tip:
Give yourself permission to cry.

How do you nurture your physical and spiritual beauty?

Love Tip:
Remember that physical beauty is skin deep, but spiritual beauty comes from love.

Write a list of things you can give away.

Love Tip:
Love knows that you define your material things; they don't define you.

What advice would you give your younger self about love?

Love Tip:
Take advice from one who has successfully learned the love lesson.

Write a love letter to yourself.

Love Tip:
You are love.

In Between Loves

#29

If what goes around comes back around, then
I'll leave the porch light on so that **love** can find me.

Love Tip:
Before you open the door to your house of love,
look through the peephole and ask, "Who's there?"

Love Note
#30

Love knows that a past **love** has passed.

Love Tip:
Focus on the present.

Love Note
#31

Love is a verb in perfect tense:
you have past loves,
you are loving someone,
and there are others waiting to be loved by you!

Love Tip:
Be presently progressive with love.

#32

Love supports you with the crutch of abstinence until you find true **love**.

Love Tip:
Get to know a person before sharing all of you.

#33

Love knows the difference between demanding and obsessive.

Love Tip:
A demanding person can be reasonable,
but an obsessive person acts unreasonably.

#34

Love balances trust and disclosure.

Love Tip:
Trust that what you seek will find you.

#35

Love knows your role in the lives of others.

Love Tip:
Pay attention to how your mate
introduces you to friends and family.

#36

Love has 20/20 vision and never turns a blind eye.

Love Tip:
Believe that who they are is who they show you,
rather than what you choose to see.

Love Note
#37

If red is associated with anger,
and red is associated with **love**,
perhaps being associated is the problem.

Love Tip:
You have the power to choose your associations.

#38

Love is not settling or difficult,
but if you continue to settle you will find it difficult to **love**.

Love Tip:
Be patient in seeking love.

Love Note
#39

Love is an action word.
In order to do well at **love**, you have to do something.

Love Tip:
Be a doer of love.

Make a list of restaurants that you would love to visit.

Love Tip: Get to know a person before sharing all of you.

Make a list of things that you want in a wo/man.

Love Tip:
Trust that what you seek will find you.

I know that I am loved when s/he ...

Love Tip:
Pay attention to how your mate introduces you to friends and family.

Describe the type of wo/man you tend to fall for most often.

Love Tip:
Believe that who they are is who they show you, rather than what you choose to see.

List social groups or organizations that you would like to join.

Love Tip:
You have the power to choose your associations.

Recall the times that love came "right on time" for you.

Love Tip:
Be patient in seeking love.

Other people know that I love them when I ...

Love Tip:
Be a doer of love.

Write a love letter to your current or future mate.

Love Tip:
Trust that what you seek will find you.

Between Lovers

#40

Love remembers how we both felt at hello.

Love Tip:
Greet each day with that same hello.

#41

Love embraces the awkward silences.

Love Tip:
Learn to listen more and speak less.

Love Note
#42

Love doesn't wait on someone to **love** you back; it loves someone even when they turn their back.

Love Tip:
You can't make someone love you.

#43

Love defies time and time heals wounds.

Love Tip:
Bandage your wounds with love.

Love Note
#44

Love is like a game of chess; in order to win, you must never compromise the king.

Love Tip:
Play to win.

Love Note
#45

Love is just a word,
until someone comes along to give it meaning.

Love Tip:
You have the power to define love.

#46

Your loving presence is the best present.

Love Tip:
Never stop reinventing yourself.
Everyone loves surprises!

#47

Love comes in 5x7, 8x10, or 24x36 for framing a perfect **love**.

Love Tip:
Visualize your picture of the perfect love.

#48

Love falls freely, trusting that s/he will catch you.

Love Tip:
Trust is the foundation of any successful relationship.

#49

The lesson in heartbreak is learning how **love** shouldn't feel.

Love Tip:
Don't try to control love.

#50

Loving you is my chief preoccupation.

Love Tip:
Focus on your mate and listen to their concerns.

#51

Loving you is like a dance.

Love Tip:
Have fun with your mate.

#52

I **love** you!

Love Tip:
It is very important to tell your mate how much you love them and what they mean to you.

Write down ways that you can say "hello" to your mate.

Love Tip:
Greet each day the way you did with the first hello.

How do you try to control love?

Love Tip:
You can't make someone love you.

Love was good for me when ...

Love Tip:
Bandage your wounds with love.

What is your source of power? How do you define love?

Love Tip:
You have the power to define love.

How would you like to reinvent yourself?

Love Tip:
Never stop reinventing yourself. Everyone loves surprises.

If I were to frame love, the picture would look like ...

Love Tip:
Visualize your picture of the perfect love.

I trust that ...

Love Tip:
Trust is the foundation of any successful relationship.

List the fun experiences you want to share with your mate.

Love Tip:
Have fun with your mate.

My mate knows I love him/her when I ...

Love Tip:
Show and tell your mate how much you love them and what they mean to you.

ACKNOWLEDGEMENTS

I would like to thank my book designer and editor, Fenesha N. Hubbard, for your countless hours and dedication. Your support helped me fulfill my dream of making *Lotario's Love Notes* a reality. Many times I felt as if you were reading my mind.

I would also like to thank all of my immediate and extended family members:

Jointer, Little-Hubbard-Romer, Taylors-Holmes-Haywood-Smith, Hall-Peace-Bell-Mitchell, Nixon, Johnson, Akins, Johnson, Brown, Washington, Thompson, Morrow, McCarthy, England, Fosters, Hill, Jackson, Lofton, Cheeks, French, Luboviski, Sims, Davis, May, Zuckerberg, Robinson, my church family at Power & Light Evangelistic Church, and my "FaceBook Family".

Most of all, I would like to thank my beautiful children--

> Lesley
> Leah,
> and
> Elijah.
>
> **I love you!**

ABOUT THE AUTHOR

Lotario D. Jointer is a divorcee with three children. He considers himself to be an ordinary man with extraordinary experiences in love. An alum of Rust College with a BS in Computer Science, he works as a financial specialist with the public school system. This is Jointer's first published work. He lives in Chicago, Illinois and is continuing his unending exploration of love.

www.LotarioJointer.com